fingering the keys

To Michael —
with gratitutde
for your interest
and support —
Reuben Jackson

fingering the keys

reuben jackson

GUT PUNCH PRESS
Cabin John, Maryland

Some of these poems appeared in *Catalyst, Gargoyle, The Indiana Review, Black American Literature Forum, The Washington Book Review, T.W.I., The Grolier Poetry Prize Annual, Washingtonian, Folio, Chelsea, Processed World, Lip Service* and a privately published chapbook entitled *Potentially Yours*.

Special thanks to C.B.

First Edition

Library of Congress
Cataloging in Publication No.: 90-86081

ISBN: 0-945144-02-4

Cover Art by Laura Costas

Gut Punch Press
PO Box 105
Cabin John, MD 20818

Production by Michael Evans

Typeset by Sunil Freeman
at the Writer's Center, Bethesda, Maryland.

This book is dedicated to all those who kept me on the field when the relative comfort of the bench and a cup or two of Gatorade seemed to be the answer. As my junior high school principal would say when implicating guilty parties over the loudspeaker, "you know who you are."

contents

III. fingering the keys

I. belly button window

on the road

(columbia, south carolina, spring 1959)

i remember enormous teepees,
neon indians dancing and dancing around them.

i did my best to convince father
that he was tired;

and that we should spend the night
at the frontier motel.

fine southern cooking
the sign said,

columbia, south carolina's best.

we could call aunt bertha,
assure her we'd arrive in augusta tomorrow,

i would spend my savings on ribbons for
maureen's hair.

it worked.

so why did he return without
room keys?

i watched the village disappear
from the backseat
of his ford.

shankman's market

"a roll of paper towels,
mr. shankman –

and a roll of necco wafers
for herschel."

he would climb that ladder
like moses ascending sinai

he joked to old ladies with
mysterious accents,

bearded men.

he was less amiable
to my brother:
clean-cut

limping
from a war wound courtesy
of hitler,

a man i heard shankman
refer to as evil

two weeks before he called my brother
boy.

albert james

albert james was black long before me
and the rest of the fellas; he was black
when black was worse than poor.

i'm talking hair that gave the finger to drugstore
pomade,
eyes red as georgia's famed clay hills.

it was 1960.
we were children.

still, his
presence in our homes was tantamount
to treason in our parent's eyes.

albert, forgive us.
we did not know about lumumba and miles davis;

neither knew nor loved any shade below
northern negro tan.

albert james was black
before nationalists
praised his shade

and extolled the benefits of fire.

i saw the flophouse where you
od'ed
likewise turn to ghost.

edward

he was an evil motherfucker
with a curveball that didn't.

his passes wobbled like the legs
of his junkie friends.

stardom eluded him
until he donned the garish colors of gangdom,

when he did,
our frightened loyalties and pocket change
were his.

but they were not enough.

he took to firing pistols in supermarkets.

the next time i saw him,
i was fast approaching manhood,

and taking shit from no one.

no matter.
he was mercedes bound.

selling love boat, reefer,
smack,

collecting dollars once again.

who killed him?

no one uttered names
once their smiles faded

like those bad pitches of his
we'd muscle in the direction of heaven.

edward never grinned;
not even when his team won by a million
runs.

even if he managed to sail a homer into the blue,
he refused to marvel at the baseball's flight.

second grade

tried to get my hair
to flop like ringo's

so i could impress
sheila watkins

whose inability
to ship kisses to england

led her to announce
that she'd settle
for a reasonable
facsimile

provided he could also play
drums

i owned a snare
and cymbal

four adjustable rings

each day i would try
forcing my locks
into action

the tight curls were
forever sleeping

i asked my barber
what he could do about this

aren't you proud of being negro
he asked

sure
i answered

but what
if sheila doesn't change her mind?

1959

those jewish boys
whose yarmulkes
gleamed like
diamonds
in sabbath
sunlight
were not allowed
to play with schvartzes.

still,
they watched our
football
games.

one day
ira checked
for elders,

darted across the asphalt,

where
for the briefest of moments,

he got a closer look.

changes

I. 1969

his father is displeased
with his three day old
stubble, another
fence between himself
and the boy
who once lay
beside him,
wanting to know
the answers to
everything.

an atheist,
he calls to the second floor
for advice:

margie –
what will we do with him:
acid rock music,
white girls,
now this!

darn
– mother
says –
i'm out of pickles.

he takes his car to
safeway;

his son cannot go.

II. 1988

sometime between
the turkey and
apple cobbler,

he mentions
that he bought
a straight razor.

no
he continues,
i'm alright.

partially or
completely?
father asks.

1973

my mother peers
over my shoulder
in search of answers

please say
you're dedicating
that poem to a woman

you don't seem to know any

listening to ella fitzgerald
does not count

so i think of someone
call her

she says the wind's
blowing from the south-southeast
at 15 miles an hour

barometer is 30.7 inches
and rising

yeah i whisper
wear that strapless french
number

see you at 8

17

too white for the
black folks,

too black for the
white folks.

comment ca va,
brothers?

the hills are alive
with the sound of
boiling
      grits.

november poem

it's the first cold november evening.
i am out driving
and there is a hitchhiker
bearing a sign
at a quiet intersection.
i ignore the cecil taylor on the radio
to read it.
perhaps they are bound for some
exciting destination,
or place that i have been.

as i drive closer, the words become legible.
DESTINATION, REUBEN JACKSON'S ARMS.
OH, HOW I MISS THEM SO.

i am jubilant, flustered.
squeal to a stop. it's donna!
i thought she was married and happy
in philadelphia.

we do not speak, but embrace.
i produce tears, she produces a butcher's knife
and quickly accomplishes her deed.

she is careful to wipe the blood
from the seatcovers,
and wipes each finger in sanitary gauze.
i still love you, she cries.
a final kiss and that still potent smile.

she still loves me, i moan before dying.
she is still neat and considerate as ever.
my pupils lock on her lovely thumb pointing northward
across the avenue.

a lonely affair

even the most die-hard liberals
have their moments;

like the man wearing the
end apartheid now button
who followed me across his bookstore;

like the woman who
interrupted me in the middle of a
poetry reading to say

she'd read tons of african-american writing,
well, alice walker.
and i had it all wrong.

she may still be there
pontificating.

i went home and watched the redskins,
pigged out on beer and nachos.

came to realize
that unlike the mass screaming
at rfk on sunday,

revolution is a lonely affair.

big chill variations

he gives me a handshake
more complicated than logarithms,

tells me my black english
has fallen on hard times,

and how he was serving molotov cocktails
to white america

while i was chasing its daughters in vermont.

a disgrace
he calls me,
a disgrace.

but still somehow
worth dinner,

a ride in his bmw,

which he swears is an acronym for
"black male warrior."

"you are the first poet
ever to dine in this club, reuben,"

"that fork is for the watercress salad."

his treat –

paid with an american express card.

gold,
but with black trim.

1975

it was a long way to go
for a party.

15 minutes from canada,
moon just above my right hand.

it was winter.
she was a schoolteacher
who smelled of jasmine.

stevie wonder sang
"looking for another pure love"
while jeff beck spun gorgeous fills
and solos.

we danced as well as our
cumbersome boots would allow.

c.

she would
gaze
through the
darkness,

whisper toward
the man
drinking
from the
center of her
body:

what are you
doing?

there were times
when i wanted
to answer.

something
witty,

out of the ordinary,

so that maybe
she'd remember

my voice.

thinking of emmett till

stars winked
above the diner
where i asked
a blonde waitress
for sugar,

and got
threatened by
a local

with
a bloodthirsty
smile.

potentially yours
(for jeff cole)

you goddamn fool,
there was always beauty within you.

your wit and
nervous laughter,

bouquets for the rainy winters
of your friends.

you who spent so much time
cursing the mirror,

envying jim rice, sonia braga,
duke ellington's lady killing charm.

why?

i think of those solos of laughter

that heaven is hearing so soon.

II. shadow dancing

52 west 8th street

(for nancy seeger)

we take sixth avenue to the village, pause
for hot dogs in washington square park,
rush past the weekend crowds on a pilgrimage.

part of my tour of new york includes pausing
at a potbellied building beside the 8th street playhouse,
nancy snaps a photograph.

jimi hendrix's studio, i mumble to passing tourists who don't
remember seeing this on their list of downtown hot spots,
and to nancy, who notices posters of jimi and mozart
in an upstairs window, snapping them just as it begins to rain.

by now i am tripping. i see a man cross macdougal
who looks like billy cox, jimi's last bassist. i am weaving like
a blue note laced with strychnine. the air smells of patchouli.
it is late august 1970.

jimi emerges from the studio, talking with a woman about
management and final mixes, which he'll supervise when
he returns from england.
i ask if he'll pause for a picture.
his turquoise belt is beautiful in the sun.

jaco

courtney
slugging a beer,
riding
shotgun.

two tone stacy adams
out the
partially open
window,

grooving to
"river people",
"punk jazz",

the percolating ostinato
in "young and fine".

we were city boys
running wild on rockwell's
canvas,

and these were our theme
songs.

"can't no
friday night
square dance band
come close to these
basslines",

he screamed into air
thick with rambling
foilage.

"we call ourselves writers,
and here we are
learning how to do it
in classrooms!"

"jaco tours the world,
makes records, headlines,

got poems in his hands."

open letter to gato
(spring 1979)

our affair is over, gato barbieri.
you have abandoned the tango
and those searing mambo themes.

herb alpert has dressed your horn
in gaudy funk arrangements,

the melodrama is gone.

who designs your album covers now? and the
liner notes about "sensuality"?
gato, you never had to say it before!

fire them all, they've buried the latin percussion
like stolen money.
were they afraid of attracting illegal aliens?

when it was humid and i felt shitty,
i'd gaze at your old eight by tens;
you were dressed in frills like a matador.

but i've thrown them all out.

a friend is coming over to play your
new record today.

i refuse to like it.

your playing on "odara" is okay i guess;
you and lani hall sound good together.

herb must have taken a leak during the mixing –
some of the old fire came through.

emotion! profits will decrease!
radio stations won't play this album!

and you will return to me a broken artist.

i will demand an apology.
a few choruses of "para mi negra"
a drum of quicas whimpering like grieving widows.

but this will not happen.
i guess i am grateful you are still around at all.
goodbye.
perhaps another lover,
or time,
will uncover your heart.

lady's way

band plays an intro
sad as the end of summer

she sings

a saxophone answers

it's shiny and tilted
like the moon

her voice
rises like sun sometimes

dips like fortune
or a mountain road

she knows
love's two faces

like i know the way to
market

and she knows
some other stuff i feel

guess that's why she's
a star

crossing the country

with a flower
for her trademark

and music
for her flame

for duke ellington

music is your mistress;
demanding constant love
and international settings.

as always, you stroll beside her.

aging, grumpy orchestra
springs into elegance at the drop
of your hand.

even so, there are casualties.

the years pass,
you bury rabbit and swee'pea,
run your fingers across the black keys,
dip the color in your hair.

cancerous nodes
rush toward a harrowing cadenza,
pen kisses paper.

a lover
in no particular hurry,
the music reveals itself
a negligee black note at a time .

i didn't know about you

(for johnny hodges)

that alto horn
could be
dreamy

unabashedly blue and
sassy

salty
like when you
go down
on a woman

lyrical as spring's
unpretentious
grandeur

its full bouquets
of brief
supple
flowers

the trip
(july 1972)

blue sky
afternoon

african robed
genius

in the
distance

performing

new lyrical
ballads

and
hip grinding
chestnuts

whose basslines
i remembered
from
father's

saturday night
with bon ton

potato chips
dip

ballantine
scotch

and beer

parties

where
someone
was always

asking for
lucille

today
stevie sings

where were you
when i needed
you

buzzy feiten
follows every
synthesized
turn

with
lovely
guitar
licks

where are
you
        randy asks

wiping
a denim
sleeve

across my
brow

ernie's tune

sometimes
your love
is like
the dark side
of singing.

handcuffs
in the form of
a smile
you offer
when surprising
me at
happy hour,

as i gossip
with a friend
whose voice is
all too rare.

time flies,
i love you more,
everything
narrows.

i am sitting
beside you
at some
testimonial dinner.

my body rumbles
with hunger

even as my stomach
is filled.

leroy

when leroy went shopping,
clothes danced off the racks,
parading before him
like call girls.

the shine
on his italian loafers
glistened clear to
naples,

not to mention
southeast d.c.

with ultra smooth
multi-syllabic words
for the ladies,

and the latest romantic albums,

he'd spread his arms
like christ of the andes,

while the rest of us mortal
brothers

put our love lives on
hold.

leroy,
cool strongman –

you still
stroll through my infrequent
recollections.

days when weekends
meant 25 cent
double features,

and you were always
first in line.

r&b

grandmother's stern interpretation
of the scriptures ruled our house,

but had no impact on our next door neighbor's penchant
for lusty tunes
by the likes of willie mae thornton
and hank ballard.

grandmother, undaunted, growled ominous warnings.
saying that the ill-fated tower of babel
was nearly as high as their backyard assemblage of
beer cans,

before god tossed mankind into chaos,

out of which grew indecipherable tongues
like those currently babbled in the name of music,

or as you young folk call it,
r&b.

battle of the bands

in this house,
lite rock
dukes it out
with charles mingus
for air space.

it is not pretty.

we rush from our respective
bunkers
to survey the damage.

a flute solo
from eric dolphy's
last tour
is drowned by the likes
of kenny rogers.

only in america,
i think to myself,

dragging those wonderful choruses
back to the basement.

in this house,
carly simon takes on
the entire ellington orchestra
and wins.

thelonious

bizarre?
mysterioso?

i say no.

for he swung like branches in march wind,

reached down
into the warm pocket of tenderness.

"little rootie tootie"
makes me dance a fat soft-shoe,

"monk's mood"
makes me sail.

but no bizarre,
no mysterioso.

he tilled song
like it was earth,

and he
a gardener
hell bent
on raising

any beauty
waiting
on the other
side.

III. fingering the keys

after the dance

are you an ethnic poet?
she asked

(eyes glued to my
zipper)

what do you mean ?
i countered

i mean
do you fry your
imagery in fatback
whose sillhouette
is illuminated
by an inner city
streetlamp
under which
several young
brothers
most of whom
will soon die or
go to prison
harmonize
until dusk
when they are
called in by
overweight heads
of households
who can cook like crazy
and are heavily

involved in the
baptist church ?

sometimes.

wrong answer,
she said sadly,

then walked away.

changing antifreeze

i know
it is only
a simple
counterclockwise
turn of the
drain valve,

but for this moment
at least,

i am not a librarian
at the mercy of mechanics,

i am my father.

i am every calloused fingered master
of automotive technology

who ever donned a shirt
with red stitch lettering
above the pocket;

call me joe.

when a neighbor passes,
i nod,
affect the pose of a man
for whom this rudimentary task
is but the beginning.

there is a space shuttle in
florida
just begging for my touch.

rochelle

i want to have
an affair
with your
poems.

take the haiku you read
on a late night
plane to chicago,

sip bourbon
with that villanelle
in a penthouse
on central park
west.

or considering
your love for this city,

an apartment above
washington
harbor.

sky dimming
like a chandelier
at twilight,

slow kisses
for each word.

sunday brunch

and where
do your parents
summer?
she asked
him.

the front porch,
he replied.

donald in love

something about
that woman
changed the way
donald screamed at
passing cement trucks.

there was a sudden passion
to his one-man conversations.

he began using felt tip markers
to write poems in the air.

wait 'till you see her,
he shouted,

then
last thursday
escorted her to the reference desk,

at which time i stood to
shake the hands of this
gale force lover.

ancient fox fur,
house slippers,
red polyester miniskirt,
orange wig.

saturday night

i'm standing in a
line

behind
a brother who
picks up a bottle
of white
zinfandel and
says:

isn't it comforting to know
that despite today's high divorce rates,
ernest and julio gallo
still get along?

21st and p

the city's
in your voice

bodegas
where it's
possible
to buy pastrami
after midnight

he pays
takes you home

turns on the tv
turns up his end
of your own
hellish rerun

i love him
you tell me

your eyes heal
behind glasses
bought in
soho

i wish you more
than expensive souvenirs

backstage

slightly tipsy,
dragging your tuxedoed escort
in my direction,

you ignored his hands
and impatience
to stand close,

tell me
that an old lover showed up
at the cotillion,

and what a wonderful kisser he still was.

i nodded,
smiled in what i hoped were
all the right places,

as your voice was lost in the swirl
of backstage chatter.

you leaned closer.

your left breast attempted
what you referred to
as an evening long fight
for liberation.

i wished i were simon bolivar.

jamal's lamentation

just last friday,
shirley
was my wife.

now she's
african-american,

turning her
afro-centric
nose up
at my spaghetti.

my mother,
whose feet are firmly
planted
in the colored camp,

says that woman's
always been fashion conscious
but little else.

grandmother is
negro,

i'd just gotten comfortable
with blackness.

guess i'm in a mixed marriage now.

a bag lady stares
at a neglected mansion
crumbling in the rain

black history month:
everyone loves your people
until march arrives.

self portrait, 1988

i am
stubborn,
broke,
but mean well,
and am trying
hard to fuse
my passions
with the world's
conventions.
but ain't no
offers for a man
capable of
singing
every solo
wayne shorter's
committed
to record
come my way.

old cape cod

if you could stand above this part of
massachusetts,

you would see how the land crooks like a
beckoning finger,

how winds have gnarled the trees.

you could follow this car to its destination,
but don't;

i could see you dropping an enormous workload
from the sky.

either that,
or a postcard which said:

dear reuben,
let me tell you about the heatwave
and string of homicides you missed.

you would coat the air above wellfleet
with muzak,

when i want to listen to coltrane,
work on my kissing,

look at the stars.

my imaginary sister gets married

you've drifted into
someone else's life,
little sister,

i feel it
each time we discuss your wedding.

we still laugh and embrace after
family dinners,

but your hands drop mine
the way they did the day you
could finally cross fifth street
without me;

you take the freeway across town.

there
the man you will marry

snores, steals the covers,
but does not call you butterball

because your youth is dead now.

he awakens full of love and promises,

whispers the blueprints
in your ear.

late october blues

if houdini returns
give him my address

loan him cab fare
tell him not to be afraid

of coming into a
colored neighborhood

'cause i need him
to make all this heartache

disappear

i need him to pull some hope
out of his silk top hat

if not i'll slight of hand

all these overdue bills
without him

transfer my daily routine

to the peace and mystery
of the grave

running, far northwest

gradations of color above bare trees:
grey, light grey
verging on blue,
dingy clouds,

dull shadows when the sun
tries to crash february's
barricades
but is turned away.

11 men breeze through calisthenics
on a nearby baseball diamond;

no one beside me
as i lumber around the track.

battle royal

this is not a beard,

it is a forest
in which my comb
snags and
pleads for mercy.

the winds do likewise
on the subway platform,

but find their way to the border
by dusk.

a month later,
i see them teasing skiers
on a "come to canada" commercial.

the tall blonde smiles
before mastering the mountain,

the woods recede
into the television.

here,
they grow thicker.

i struggle like
a weary boxer
to get out.

martha

they say there are no
blues singers in the suburbs.
i witness you
and those small scratches upside
the face of loneliness.
desperation disguised
as an evening with friends from
what were not always such distant
places: downtown, far
northwest.

dinner seems to have more courses than grad school.
dessert shuffles toward the veranda,
forgets something in the bathroom,
or was it the y on 12th street,
changes its mind,
and occupies the space between us,

an angel food barrier
you quietly shove aside.

june 1st

depression is to poetry

as heroin is to
be-bop:

an unromantic
deterrent.

kids,
don't try this at home.

fingering the keys

because i am fond of
plastic razors,

i cannot help
but recall
mornings below
father's shadow,

listening to fresh stubble
go willingly.

a delicious rustle
i would associate with autumn,

before my own disguise
was ripe for harvest.

now kathleen
has no place to hide her fingers,

and reminds me of her loneliness.

but today
i am back beside the
master soloist,

a protege quietly
fingering the keys.

in a silent way

josef's wife
takes the children
out into snowy
vienna

once they are gone
his childhood knocks

rolls in a cart
bearing
recollections

strong enough to
drive him to
music

when he returns to america
it is written

a saxophonist from
new orleans
meets josef
a bassist
and percussionist
in a studio in
new york

nine years later

i hear the result
in a friends
house

outside cambridge
massachusetts

she wants to order
szechuan

i want the peace
that shepherd boy

heard across the
sea

Crystal Banks

Biography

A native of Augusta, Georgia, Reuben Jackson has been a resident of Washington, D.C. since 1959, where he lives with his wife, Jackie, currently works as an archivist with the Smithsonian Institution's Duke Ellington Collection, and is a member of the poetry group Lip Service.

His other passions include pedestrian attempts at blues guitar majesty, baseball, the music of Jimi Hendrix, Billie Holiday, Miles Davis, Marvin Gaye, and Cecil Taylor, the poetry of Frank O'Hara, and New York City. This is his first book.